Common Core Creativity:

Language Arts Fun in the Classroom!

30 Projects and Activities for Middle School ELA

Garrett M. Carter

Printed by CreateSpace

Background story

More so now than ever, teachers are tasked with helping students develop and enhance skills, demonstrate mastery of these skills, and show growth from previous years. Teachers are being held accountable for student growth in unprecedented ways. In the midst of all of this change, it is extremely important to remember that we can, and must, find creative ways to reach, teach, and engage students. The goal of this book is to promote student learning and growth through creative, fun, and effective standards-based projects and activities.

How to use this book

The user-friendly table of contents lists the projects/activities, page numbers, and related standards. The introductory pages contain a brief description of all projects and activities. With a different intent, or slight modification, you may find that additional standards apply. At the time of this publication, over 40 states have adopted the English Language Arts Standards as determined by the Common Core State Standards Initiative. However, to ensure that you get the most out of each project and activity, cross reference the materials from this book with the standards for your state.

Why this book?
- Standards-based
- Promotes collaboration
- Engaging
- Fun
- Relevant

Also by this author

Not an Oxymoron: Standards-Based Fun in the Classroom! 30 Projects and Activities for Middle School Language Arts (2011)

Common Core Galore: Language Arts Fun in the Classroom! 30 Activities for Middle School ELA (2015)

This book is dedicated to the students we teach and inspire...and the students who teach and inspire us.

Table of Contents & Alignment of Standards*	Page(s)	Reading: Literature	Reading: Informational Text	Writing	Speaking & Listening	Language
Project/Activity Name:						
Project and Activity Introductions	1					
Character Apps	5	X		X		
Plot Photo Gallery	9	X		X		
Vocabulary Your Way-Homework and Quiz	11	X	X			X
Vocabulary Your Way-Homework	12	X	X			X
Making and Supporting an Argument or Claim	13	X	X	X		
Highlighting Important Information	15	X				X
Theme and Central Idea Development	16	X				
Character Decks	17	X		X		
Literature Calendar	19	X	X	X		
Name that Show	21	X		X		
Flip it! Author's Purpose: Entertain and Inform	22		X	X		
Flip it! Author's Purpose: Entertain and Persuade	23		X	X		
Flip it! Author's Purpose: Inform and Persuade	24		X	X		
Effective Discussions	25				X	
Like an Animal	27	X		X		
Act it Out: Characterization	28	X		X	X	X
Act it Out: Theme	29	X		X	X	X
Act it Out: Mood	30	X		X	X	X
Character Playlist	31	X		X		
Character Pie	32	X		X		
History and Fiction	33	X		X		
Setting and Story	34	X		X		
Point of View	35	X	X	X		
Comparing and Contrasting Newspaper Articles	37		X	X		
Newspaper Response	39		X	X		
Audience on a Roll	40		X	X		
Character Report Card	41	X		X		
Musical Text	42	X		X	X	X
Word Study	43					X
Words to Live By	44		X	X		

*All of the projects and activities included in this book are standards-based and/or support skill development of the English Language Arts Standards as determined by the Common Core State Standards Initiative. To ensure these projects and activities support your curriculum, refer to the English Language Arts Standards for grade-specific information. This book has not been evaluated, reviewed, or endorsed by the Common Core State Standards Initiative.

Project and Activity Introductions

Character Apps (pgs. 5-8)
This activity allows students to use their love of technology and apply it to a character from a text they are reading. Students will use their knowledge of a character to determine what apps that character is likely to have on his/her smartphone. Students have to support their claims with explanations. This activity works great in class or as an assigned project.

Plot Photo Gallery (pgs. 9-10)
Students create a photo gallery on a smartphone-styled graphic organizer to illustrate and explain the plot of a novel.

Vocabulary Your Way-Homework and Quiz (pg. 11)
The teacher partners with students to identify appropriate words on which students are tested. Students first submit the paper as homework. The teacher then selects words that students must learn for the quiz. After a little cutting, the same paper actually becomes the quiz, complete with an answer key. This activity is a great tool to use for differentiated instruction.

Vocabulary Your Way-Homework (pg. 12)
Students take center stage at identifying their own vocabulary words instead of working from the same list of words as their peers. With this version of the assignment, there is no quiz involved. Again, this is a great way to differentiate instruction.

Making and Supporting an Argument or Claim (pgs. 13-14)
Students identify an argument or claim in the text and support it using evidence from the text. This activity also helps students learn to track information as it develops over the course of the text.

Highlighting Important Information (pg. 15)
Many standardized tests are prompting students to highlight specific lines in the text that contain or support information. This activity allows students to practice this skill. Teachers must place a text in the box before distributing to students. Teachers must also instruct students which literary terms they should look for in the passage. If there are other terms you would like students to find, have them write those terms on the blank lines.

Theme and Central Idea Development (pg. 16)
Students identify a theme or central idea and analyze its development over the text. Students ultimately judge the author's effectiveness.

Character Decks (pgs. 17-18)

Students use card deck values to determine major and minor characters from the text. High card values should be used for major characters. Students justify claims with evidence from the text. As an extension activity, students may develop a card game incorporating characters from the text.

Literature Calendar (pgs. 19-20)

Students chart the development of a theme or central idea from the text. The front of the paper involves symbolism and the back involves explanation and analysis. This may be used for fictional or nonfictional texts.

Name that Show (pg. 21)

Students identify a television show and explain why a character from the text would relate to that show. After creating an illustration, students summarize the show and support their claims.

Flip it! Author's Purpose (Entertain and Inform, Entertain and Persuade, Inform and Persuade) (pgs. 22-24)

With these activities, students practice identifying an author's purpose based on the flip of a coin. Instead of dictating to students how many of each scenario to create, you simply let the coin decide. Once students have completed the activity, they should trade papers with a partner for additional practice.

Effective Discussions (pgs. 25-26)

Students come to class prepared to engage in productive discussions with their peers. The front of the paper needs to be completed prior to the discussion while the back is completed during the discussion to promote active listening.

Like an Animal (pg. 27)

This activity involves students determining what animals could symbolize characters from the text. Students state their claims, create illustrations, and support their claims based on textual evidence.

Act it Out (Characterization, Theme, Mood) (pgs. 28-30)

Students work collaboratively to develop skits that convey characterization, theme, and mood. After completing the paper, students begin practicing for their performance.

Character Playlist (pg. 31)

Students imagine what songs would be on the playlist of a character from the text. Students may be tempted to include songs that they themselves enjoy, but encourage them to focus on songs that may speak to what their character has experienced. Students should reference the text in their explanations. As an extension activity, students may present songs and explanations to the class.

Character Pie (pg. 32)
Students create pie graphs based on a character's personality traits. Students must support their claims with reasoning from the text. Extension activities may include having students complete this assignment on paper plates and attaching construction paper for the crust. Students may also develop comprehension questions based on the pie graph to be answered by a partner.

History and Fiction (pg. 33)
Students first complete a journal entry recalling a recent personal experience. Once the journal is completed, students alter the story by incorporating fictional elements. Students reflect upon the way in which authors may use or alter history in their works.

Setting and Story (pg. 34)
Setting plays an integral role in many stories. This activity encourages students to think about the interactions among the setting, characters, and plot of a text. Students are also challenged to determine how the text would be different in another setting.

Point of View (pgs. 35-36)
This activity causes students to look at an event or situation in the text from multiple points of view. Students are also tasked to compare and contrast the different points of view.

Comparing and Contrasting Newspaper Articles (pgs. 37-38)
Students examine two different news articles on the same topic. In addition to comparing and contrasting the information, students determine if claims are well supported and which article is more effective.

Newspaper Response (pg. 39)
Students use a newspaper article to develop and enhance skills related to informational text.

Audience on a Roll (pg. 40)
Students roll a die and then create a short description of a type of literature with a specific audience in mind. Once students have completed all descriptions, they should trade papers with a partner for additional practice.

Character Report Card (pg. 41)
Instead of students receiving a report card, they are completing one. Students choose a character from the text and identify several personality traits on which to grade the character. Students must use page references from the text to provide evidence of the character's progress.

Musical Text (pg. 42)
Books are not the only way in which stories are told. Songs also tell stories. Students listen to a song and determine its summary, theme, mood, etc. This works great as an in-class activity or homework assignment.

Word Study (pg. 43)
Students use a variety of ways to master new words.

Words to Live By (pg. 44)
Students research quotes that are relevant to areas of their lives. Students select a quote and examine it in multiple ways. As an extension activity, students may present their quotes to the class and explain the meaning.

Be sure to view the BONUS SECTION at the end of the book!

Character Apps

Name:_____ Period:_____

<u>Directions</u>: Fill in the smartphone below with apps that a character from the text might have on his/her phone. All app boxes must be colored. Make connections to the text as you decide what apps this character might have. For example, if a character likes to read, he or she may have a reading app downloaded. On the pages that follow, use evidence from the text to explain why you chose the apps that you did.

This phone belongs to:_____

1.	2.	3.	4.
5.	6.	7.	8.
9.	10.	11.	12.
13.	14.	15.	16.

Character Apps

1. Name of app: _____

Explanation of why this character might have this app: _____

_____

_____

2. Name of app: _____

Explanation of why this character might have this app: _____

_____

_____

3. Name of app: _____

Explanation of why this character might have this app: _____

_____

_____

4. Name of app: _____

Explanation of why this character might have this app: _____

_____

_____

5. Name of app: _____

Explanation of why this character might have this app: _____

_____

_____

6. Name of app: _____

Explanation of why this character might have this app: _____

_____

_____

Character Apps

7. Name of app: _____

Explanation of why this character might have this app: _____

_____

_____

8. Name of app: _____

Explanation of why this character might have this app: _____

_____

_____

9. Name of app: _____

Explanation of why this character might have this app: _____

_____

_____

10. Name of app: _____

Explanation of why this character might have this app: _____

_____

_____

11. Name of app: _____

Explanation of why this character might have this app: _____

_____

_____

12. Name of app: _____

Explanation of why this character might have this app: _____

_____

_____

Character Apps

13. Name of app: _____

Explanation of why this character might have this app: _____

_____

_____

14. Name of app: _____

Explanation of why this character might have this app: _____

_____

_____

15. Name of app: _____

Explanation of why this character might have this app: _____

_____

_____

16. Name of app: _____

Explanation of why this character might have this app: _____

_____

_____

Explain why you chose this character to complete the project. Did you find this task easy or difficult? Explain your answers.

_____

_____

_____

_____

_____

_____

_____

_____

_____

Plot Photo Gallery

Name:_____ Period:_____

Directions: Imagine that a camera from a smartphone captured a picture of a scene from each part of the novel's plot. Draw and color these scenes below in the phone's photo gallery. On the back of this paper, explain each scene.

Novel:_____

Exposition	Initiating Conflict
Rising Action	Climax
Falling Action	Resolution

Plot Photo Gallery

Exposition:

_____
_____
_____
_____
_____

Initiating Conflict:

_____
_____
_____
_____
_____

Rising Action:

_____
_____
_____
_____
_____

Climax:

_____
_____
_____
_____
_____

Falling Action:

_____
_____
_____
_____
_____

Resolution:

_____
_____
_____
_____
_____

Vocabulary Your Way-Homework and Quiz

Name:_____   Period:_____

<u>Directions</u>: In the left column, write the vocabulary word you identified and the page number where you found it. In the middle column, record what you think is the definition of the word. In the right column, use a dictionary to define the word. This paper will first be collected as homework, and I will check the boxes on the far left side of the paper for the words you will be responsible for defining on your vocabulary quiz. I will then return this paper to you and on the day of the quiz, you will cut along the dotted lines and staple just these directions and the vocabulary words to a clean sheet of notebook paper. You will then take the quiz by defining the checked words from this paper on your notebook paper. After the quiz, the portion of this paper that was cut out will be collected and the right column will serve as the answer key.

Teacher Use: ⇩

	Vocabulary word & Page #:	What you think the word means:	Definition of the word:
☐	1.		
☐	2.		
☐	3.		
☐	4.		
☐	5.		
☐	6.		
☐	7.		
☐	8.		
☐	9.		
☐	10.		
☐	11.		
☐	12.		
☐	13.		
☐	14.		
☐	15.		

Vocabulary Your Way-Homework

Name:_____   Period:_____

Directions: In the left column, write the vocabulary word you identified and the page number where you found it. In the middle column, record what you think is the definition of the word. In the right column, use a dictionary to define the word.

Vocabulary word & Page #:	What you think the word means:	Definition of the word:
1.		
2.		
3.		
4.		
5.		
6.		
7.		
8.		
9.		
10.		
11.		
12.		
13.		
14.		
15.		

Making and Supporting an Argument or Claim

Name:_____   Period:_____

Directions: In the boxes below, cite textual evidence to support an argument or claim from the text. For example, if the claim is that a character is naïve, your pieces of textual evidence should support this claim. Additional prompts are on the back of this paper.

Argument or Claim:

=

Textual Evidence 1:   Page #/Paragraph:

Explanation:

+

Textual Evidence 2:   Page #/Paragraph:

Explanation:

+

Textual Evidence 3:   Page #/Paragraph:

Explanation:

Textual Evidence 1

Decide if evidence is sufficient to support argument or claim. Explain.

_____

_____

_____

_____

_____

Textual Evidence 2

Decide if evidence is sufficient to support argument or claim. Explain.

_____

_____

_____

_____

_____

Textual Evidence 3

Decide if evidence is sufficient to support argument or claim. Explain.

_____

_____

_____

_____

_____

Highlighting Important Information

Name:_____   Period:_____

<u>Directions</u>: Read the text in the box below. Highlight examples of the following literary terms found in the passage:

theme   foreshadowing   conflict   flashback   simile   metaphor

personification   characterization   inference   point of view   irony

other: _____   _____   _____   _____

On the back of this paper, choose three literary terms that you highlighted in the passage and explain how each contributes to the text.

Theme and Central Idea Development

Name:_____   Period:_____

Directions: Identify a theme or central idea from the text. In the boxes below, track its development over the course of the text. Determine if the author was effective in conveying the theme or central idea. Explain.

Theme/Central Idea:

Initial Development:

Continued Development:

Final Development:

Effectiveness of author conveying theme or central idea:

16

Character Decks

Name:_____   Period:_____

<u>Directions</u>: Using the cards below, assign two major characters from the text a value based on their roles in the text. Write the character's name and card value on each card, and then draw and color a picture of the character. Support your claims with reasoning and evidence from text. On the back of this paper, follow the same instructions for two minor characters.

Major Character

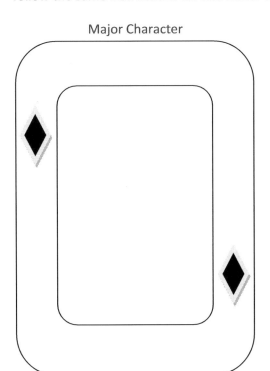

Major Character

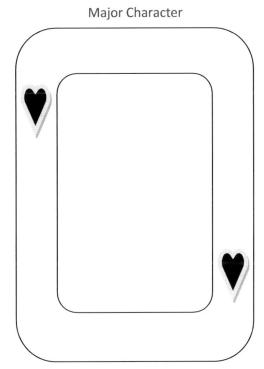

Minor Character

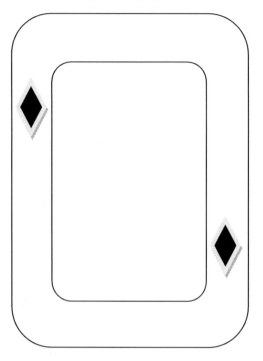

_____

_____

_____

_____

_____

_____

_____

_____

_____

Minor Character

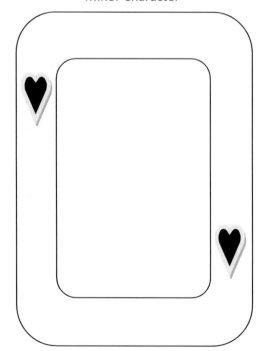

_____

_____

_____

_____

_____

_____

_____

_____

_____

Literature Calendar

Name:_____   Period:_____

Directions: Identify a theme or central idea of the text. Use the calendar below to mark three to five events that helped to develop the theme or central idea over the course of the text. Mark events by illustrating a symbol, and then explain all symbols and developments on the back of this paper. If specific dates are not specified in the text, create your own.

Text:_____

◀	**Calendar**			▶	+
	Month		**Year**		

Sun	Mon	Tue	Wed	Thu	Fri	Sat

Theme or Central Idea:_____

_____

Event 1: _____
Symbol: _____
Explanation of symbol: _____
_____

How this contributes to the development of the theme or central idea: _____
_____
_____
_____

Event 2: _____
Symbol: _____
Explanation of symbol: _____
_____

How this contributes to the development of the theme or central idea: _____
_____
_____
_____

Event 3: _____
Symbol: _____
Explanation of symbol: _____
_____

How this contributes to the development of the theme or central idea: _____
_____
_____
_____

Event 4: _____
Symbol: _____
Explanation of symbol: _____
_____

How this contributes to the development of the theme or central idea: _____
_____
_____
_____

Event 5: _____
Symbol: _____
Explanation of symbol: _____
_____

How this contributes to the development of the theme or central idea: _____
_____
_____
_____

Name that Show

Name:_____   Period:_____

Directions: Identify a television show and explain why a character from the text would relate to the show. Create an illustration for the show, and then answer the questions below.

Show name:_____
Character:_____

Summarize the central idea of the television show.

_____
_____
_____
_____

Explain why the character would relate to this show. Use evidence from the text to support your claim.

_____
_____
_____
_____
_____
_____
_____

Flip it! Author's Purpose: Entertain and Inform

Name:_____   Period:_____

Directions: Flip a coin 10 times. Record each flip on the chart below. "H" is for heads and "T" is for tails. For every heads you flip, write a sentence that shows the author's purpose is to entertain an audience. For every tails you flip, write a sentence that shows the author's purpose is to inform an audience. After all of your sentences are completed, trade papers with a partner. **Fold the paper so your partner cannot see where you recorded your flips.** In the last column, your partner will write "E" if the sentence entertains and "I" if the sentence informs. An example has been completed for you.

H or T: ⇩	Sentence:	E or I:
T	An article in a science magazine that explains photosynthesis.	I

⇧

Fold Here

22

Name:_____   Period:_____

Directions: Flip a coin 10 times. Record each flip on the chart below. "H" is for heads and "T" is for tails. For every heads you flip, write a sentence that shows the author's purpose is to entertain an audience. For every tails you flip, write a sentence that shows the author's purpose is to persuade an audience. After all of your sentences are completed, trade papers with a partner. **Fold the paper so your partner cannot see where you recorded your flips.** In the last column, your partner will write "E" if the sentence entertains and "P" if the sentence persuades. An example has been completed for you.

H or T:	Sentence:	E or P:
H	A comic book about a magical polar bear that attends middle school.	E

Fold Here

Flip it! Author's Purpose: Inform and Persuade

Name:_____   Period:_____

Directions: Flip a coin 10 times. Record each flip on the chart below. "H" is for heads and "T" is for tails. For every heads you flip, write a sentence that shows the author's purpose is to inform an audience. For every tails you flip, write a sentence that shows the author's purpose is to persuade an audience. After all of your sentences are completed, trade papers with a partner. **Fold the paper so your partner cannot see where you recorded your flips.** In the last column, your partner will write "I" if the sentence informs and "P" if the sentence persuades. An example has been completed for you.

H or T: ⇓   Sentence: I or P:

H or T	Sentence	I or P
T	An editorial in the local newspaper urging the city to hire more firefighters.	P

⇑

Fold Here

Effective Discussions

Name:_____   Period:_____

Directions: Complete the boxes below so that you are prepared to engage in a productive class discussion. Complete the back of this paper on the day of the discussion.

Issue or topic:_____

Initial position on issue or topic:

$$\boxed{}$$

Three reasons for your position and/or supporting claims:

Three questions you have on the issue or topic:

$$\boxed{}$$

$$\boxed{}$$

$$\boxed{}$$

New information you learned:

Observations while working with peers:

Final position on issue or topic:

Name:_____   Period:_____

Directions: In each box, draw and color an animal that is representative of a character from the text. For example, an animal that is known for being loyal might be compared to a character in the text that shows loyalty. Above each box, state your claim. Next to each box, explain why you linked the character and animal using information from the text.

Claim:

_____ is like a(n) _____.

_____

_____

_____

_____

_____

_____

_____

_____

_____

_____

Claim:

_____ is like a(n) _____.

_____

_____

_____

_____

_____

_____

_____

_____

_____

_____

Claim:

_____ is like a(n) _____.

_____

_____

_____

_____

_____

_____

_____

_____

_____

_____

Act it Out: Characterization

Names:_____

_____

_____ Period:_____

Directions: Students work in small groups to create skits that reveal the personalities of at least two characters. In the skit, the personality traits cannot be directly stated. Instead, the audience must be able to identify the personality traits based on the plot, dialogue, and actions of the characters in the skit.

Example: Perhaps in your skit, a student is bullying a little kid. One person interrupts the bullying, chastises the bully, and makes sure that the little kid is okay. From this skit, one could characterize the person who stopped the bully as brave because he confronted the bully. This character could also be characterized as caring since he checked on the victim. The bully could be characterized as malicious because he found pleasure in making fun of a little kid.

Now it's your turn! Below, provide a summary of your skit. Also, identify two characterizations that your audience is likely to identify after watching your group's performance. Explain your answers.

Summary:

_____
_____
_____
_____
_____
_____
_____
_____
_____

Characterizations:

Name/Description of Character 1: _____

Personality trait revealed:_____

Explanation:_____
_____

Name/Description of Character 2: _____

Personality trait revealed:_____

Explanation:_____
_____

Names:_____

_____

_____ Period:_____

Directions: Students work in small groups to create skits that reveal themes. In the skit, the themes cannot be directly stated. Instead, the audience must be able to identify the themes based on the plot, dialogue, and actions of the characters in the skit.

Example: Perhaps in your skit, a girl tells a boy that she will never be his girlfriend because he is too short. Later in life, the short boy grows into a tall man with a wonderful wife and two kids. The girl, on the other hand, grows into a very lonely woman. From this skit, themes could include: don't judge a book by its cover, you may regret some decisions later in life, etc.

Now it's your turn! Below, provide a summary of your skit. Also, identify two themes that your audience is likely to identify after watching your group's performance. Explain your answers.

Summary:

_____

_____

_____

_____

_____

_____

_____

_____

_____

Themes:

Theme 1:

_____

_____

Explanation:_____

_____

_____

Theme 2:

_____

_____

Explanation:_____

_____

_____

Names:_____

_____

_____ Period:_____

Directions: Students work in small groups to create skits that convey a mood to the audience. In the skit, the mood cannot be directly stated. Instead, the audience must be able to identify the mood based on the plot, dialogue, and actions of the characters in the skit.

Example: Perhaps in your skit, a mother and father have to explain to their children that their dog has died. The children are devastated by the news and cry hysterically. The audience is able to determine that the mood of the skit is sad.

Now it's your turn! Below, provide a summary of your skit. Also, identify and explain the mood that your audience is likely to identify after watching your group's performance.

Summary:

_____
_____
_____
_____
_____
_____
_____
_____
_____
_____
_____
_____

Mood: _____

Explanation:_____
_____
_____
_____
_____
_____
_____
_____
_____
_____
_____
_____
_____
_____

Character Playlist

Name:_____   Period:_____

Directions: Choose five songs that a character from the text would likely have in a playlist. Think about songs that offer advice or share similarities with situations that the character has experienced. Below, record the songs and artists. On the back of this paper, explain your song selections (3-5 sentences per song).

Text:_____

Character:_____

Playlist

1. Song: Artist:	
2. Song: Artist:	
3. Song: Artist:	
4. Song: Artist:	
5. Song: Artist:	

Character Pie

Name:_____   Period:_____

<u>Directions</u>: Create a pie graph below based on the personality traits of a character in the text. Create a legend and color when finished. On the back of this paper, explain the traits and percentages using clear reasoning and relevant evidence from the text.

Text:_____

Character:_____

Legend:

Name:_____   Period:_____

Directions: In Box 1, write five sentences describing a recent personal experience. Include critical details such as names, places, dates, and other relevant information.

Box 1

```



```

In Box 2, alter the story from Box 1 so that it now includes fictional information.

Box 2

```



```

Identify and explain a purpose and audience for each story.

_____
_____
_____

Explain how real life events might impact fictional stories.

_____
_____
_____

Explain why authors might use or alter history to create fictional stories.

_____
_____
_____

Name:_____   Period:_____

Directions: In the box below, illustrate the setting of the text. Next to the box, explain how the setting influences the characters or plot.

[illustration box]

_____
_____
_____
_____
_____
_____
_____
_____
_____
_____
_____
_____

In the box below, create a completely new setting (different place, time period, etc.) for the same text. Next to the box, explain how this new setting influences the characters or plot. In other words, explain how the text from above is impacted by this new setting.

[illustration box]

_____
_____
_____
_____
_____
_____
_____
_____
_____
_____
_____
_____

Point of View

Name:_____   Period:_____

Directions: In the rectangular box, summarize an event or situation from the text. In the speech bubbles, provide the point of view of four individuals from the text in relation to this event or situation. After finishing this side of the paper, complete the prompts on the back.

Individual A: _____

Individual B: _____

Event or situation:

Individual C: _____

Individual D: _____

Individual A: _____
Explanation of this individual's point of view: _____
_____
_____
_____

Compare and contrast Individual A's point of view with Individual B's point of view: _____
_____
_____
_____
_____

Individual B: _____
Explanation of this individual's point of view: _____
_____
_____
_____

Compare and contrast Individual B's point of view with Individual C's point of view: _____
_____
_____
_____
_____

Individual C: _____
Explanation of this individual's point of view: _____
_____
_____
_____

Compare and contrast Individual C's point of view with Individual D's point of view: _____
_____
_____
_____
_____

Individual D: _____
Explanation of this individual's point of view: _____
_____
_____
_____

Compare and contrast Individual D's point of view with Individual A's point of view: _____
_____
_____
_____
_____

Comparing and Contrasting Newspaper Articles

Name:_____   Period:_____

Directions: For this activity, you need two newspaper articles on the same event. Look for world or national news appearing in both national and local papers. Additional prompts are on the back.

Article 1:_____   Article 2: _____
Name of newspaper:_____   Name of newspaper:_____

Record article information next to bullet points to show development of central ideas.

O

O

O

O

O

O

O

O

O

O

Comparing and Contrasting Newspaper Articles

1. Determine two or more central ideas in the articles.

_____
_____
_____
_____
_____
_____

2. Compare and contrast the organizational structures of the articles.

_____
_____
_____
_____
_____
_____

3. Compare and contrast the authors' points of view and purpose.

_____
_____
_____
_____
_____
_____

4. Decide if claims are supported by sound reasoning and relevant evidence.

_____
_____
_____
_____
_____
_____

5. Decide which article was more effective in conveying the central idea.

_____
_____
_____
_____
_____
_____

Newspaper Response

Name:_____   Period:_____

Directions: Read a newspaper article and then answer the following questions.

1. Identify the title of the article. _____
_____

2. Identify the subtitle of the article. _____
_____

3. Summarize the article. _____
_____
_____
_____
_____

4. Identify a source that contributed to the article._____
_____

5. Identify one fact presented in the article. _____
_____

6. Develop an opinion based on the article._____
_____
_____

7. Identify a cause and effect relationship based on information in the article._____
_____
_____
_____

8. Determine if there is bias in the article. Explain. _____
_____
_____
_____

9. Decide how television news coverage of this same topic might differ from this newspaper article.
_____
_____
_____
_____

10. Draw a symbol related to the article and explain its meaning.

                    Symbol   Meaning

Name:_____   Period:_____

Directions: Roll a die 10 times. Record each roll on the chart below. Based on the number rolled, write a brief description of a type of literature which targets that audience. After all of your descriptions are completed, trade papers with a partner. **Fold the paper so your partner cannot see where you recorded your rolls.** In the last column, your partner will determine the intended audience. An example has been completed for you.

1: Young Children   2: Teen Boys   3. Teen Girls   4. College Students   5. Adults   6. Senior Citizens

Roll #: ⇩	Description of Literature	Audience:
6	An advertisement promoting move-in specials at a new retirement community.	Senior Citizens

⇧
Fold Here

Name:_____   Period:_____

<u>Directions</u>: Complete the report card below using a character from the text. Identify each character trait and then determine a grade. Use evidence from the text to support your answer. Cite page numbers containing textual evidence.

Character Report Card	
Character Name:	**Date:**
Text:	
Character Trait:	**Grade:**
Evidence of Progress:	**Page Reference:**
Character Trait:	**Grade:**
Evidence of Progress:	**Page Reference:**
Character Trait:	**Grade:**
Evidence of Progress:	**Page Reference:**
Character Trait:	**Grade:**
Evidence of Progress:	**Page Reference:**
Character Trait:	**Grade:**
Evidence of Progress:	**Page Reference:**

Name:_____   Period:_____

Directions: Listen to a song and read the lyrics while the song plays. At the end of the song, complete this worksheet.

1. Record the name of the song.
_____

2. Record the artist.
_____

3. Summarize the song.
_____
_____

4. Identify and explain a theme from the song.
_____
_____

5. Identify and explain the tone of the song.
_____
_____

6. Identify and explain the mood of the song.
_____
_____

7. Identify an example of figurative language in the song. Explain its meaning.
_____
_____

8. Identify and explain the genre this song would have as a book.
_____
_____

9. Compare and contrast this song with a song by a different artist on the same topic.
_____
_____
_____
_____

10. Draw a symbol related to the song and explain its meaning.

Symbol   Meaning

Name:_____   Period:_____

Directions: Choose four vocabulary words from the text and complete the information below.

Word:_____
Page #:_____   Pronunciation:_____
Affix or root clues/What you think the word means:_____
Sentence from the text:_____
_____
Definition:_____
Synonym:_____   Antonym: _____
New sentence:_____
_____

Word:_____
Page #:_____   Pronunciation:_____
Affix or root clues/What you think the word means:_____
Sentence from the text:_____
_____
Definition:_____
Synonym:_____   Antonym: _____
New sentence:_____
_____

Word:_____
Page #:_____   Pronunciation:_____
Affix or root clues/What you think the word means:_____
Sentence from the text:_____
_____
Definition:_____
Synonym:_____   Antonym: _____
New sentence:_____
_____

Word:_____
Page #:_____   Pronunciation:_____
Affix or root clues/What you think the word means:_____
Sentence from the text:_____
_____
Definition:_____
Synonym:_____   Antonym: _____
New sentence:_____
_____

Name:_____   Period:_____

Directions: After researching famous quotes, choose one quote that you believe offers good advice and can be applied to several areas of your life. Record that quote below and answer the prompts that follow.

Quote:

_____

_____

_____

Source:

_____

Determine the quote's literal and figurative meanings.

_____

_____

_____

Identify the quote's central idea.

_____

_____

_____

Determine this author's point of view based on the quote.

_____

_____

_____

Explain how this author's point of view distinguishes him or her from others.

_____

_____

_____

Find another quote by a different person on the same topic. Record that quote below and include the source.

_____

_____

Compare and contrast the quotes. Analyze how word choice, point of view, information, and interpretation shaped the development of different conclusions on the same topic.

_____

_____

_____

_____

_____

_____

BONUS SECTION

Includes:

- A project from the author's first book, *Not an Oxymoron: Standards-Based Fun in the Classroom! 30 Projects and Activities for Middle School Language Arts*
- A classroom management system developed by the author
- A daily theme activity that keeps each week moving along

Disney Movie Project

In order to complete this assignment, you will need to watch **one** animated Disney movie. Movie options will be determined by your teacher. After selecting your movie, complete these worksheets while you view the film. If you do not have the movie you wish to use, ask your parent or guardian for assistance in obtaining it.

1. Design a front cover and attach it to these pages. Include artwork and the name of the movie. Also, include your name, the assignment title, your class period, and the date.

2. Label the plot diagram below by placing the following terms in order: resolution, rising action, initiating conflict, falling action, exposition, climax

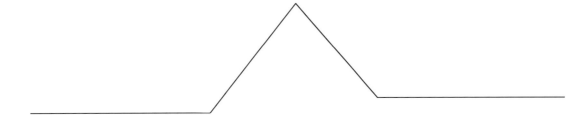

3. In the boxes below, <u>label and explain</u> each part of the movie's plot (the first box is labeled for you).

Exposition		

Disney Movie Project

<u>Directions</u>: Write the definition of each *italicized* word and then answer the questions that follow.

Answer all questions in complete sentences (this does not apply to definitions).

4. *Protagonist-*_____

Who is the protagonist?_____

Do you like this character? Why or why not?_____

_____

5. *Antagonist-*_____

Who is the antagonist?_____

Do you like this character? Why or why not?_____

_____

6. *Conflict-*_____

Explain the conflict between the protagonist and the antagonist._____

_____

_____

_____

7. *Foreshadowing-*_____

Is there foreshadowing in this movie?   Yes   No

If so, explain. If not, provide your own example._____

_____

_____

_____

Disney Movie Project

8. *Flashback-*_____

Is there a flashback in this movie?   Yes   No

If so, explain. If not, provide your own example._____

_____

_____

_____

9. *Personification-*_____

Is there personification in this movie?   Yes   No

If so, explain. If not, provide your own example._____

_____

_____

_____

10. *Mood-*_____

Describe a scene from this movie and explain the mood._____

_____

_____

_____

11. *Theme-*_____

Explain a theme found in this movie._____

_____

_____

_____

Disney Movie Project

12. *Characterization-*_____

Describe a scene in which a character's personality is revealed._____

_____

_____

_____

13. *Simile-*_____

Is there a simile in this movie?   Yes   No

If so, write and explain the simile. If not, provide your own example._____

_____

_____

_____

14. *Metaphor-*_____

Is there a metaphor in this movie?   Yes   No

If so, write and explain the metaphor. If not, provide your own example._____

_____

_____

_____

15. *Symbolism-*_____

In the spaces below, draw symbols that represent the protagonist and the antagonist.

          Protagonist   Antagonist

The Disney Movie Project and many other projects and activities can be found in the author's first book, *Not an Oxymoron: Standards-Based Fun in the Classroom! 30 Projects and Activities for Middle School Language Arts*. This book promotes skill development of the English Language Arts Standards as determined by the Common Core State Standards Initiative.

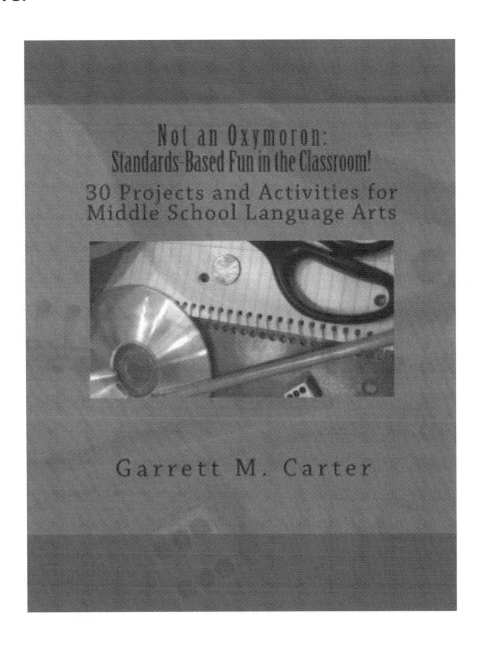

Classroom Management Plan: Class of the Quarter

Middle school students love competition! I created a Class of the Quarter system to reward the class that receives the most points by the end of the quarter.

Classes are scored on:
- Coming to class on time
- Being prepared
- Beginning the First Five (bell work) immediately upon hearing the bell
- Having excellent behavior
- Having excellent participation

The rubric is on the following page. It is very straightforward and students understand exactly how they are being scored. I post scores daily, and below you can see how I track this information.

Students become very interested in who is leading the competition. Students often direct other students to stay on task. At the end of the quarter, the class with the most points earns a Class of the Quarter party! I feed the class and allow students to plan the day (within reason). Students may bring in games, movies, etc. I also give students a homework pass that they may use the next quarter. Most of all, students love having bragging rights!

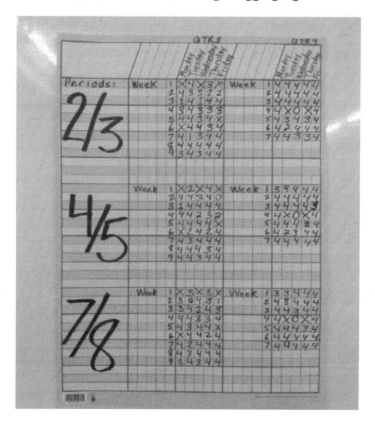

Rubric for Class of the Quarter:

A (4 points)
90-100% of students come to class on time, prepared, and immediately begin working on the First Five. Behavior/participation of students is excellent.

B (3 points)
80-89% of students come to class on time, prepared, and immediately begin working on the First Five. Behavior/participation of students is above average.

C (2 points)
70-79% of students come to class on time, prepared, and immediately begin working on the First Five. Behavior/participation of students is average.

D (1 point)
60-69% of students come to class on time, prepared, and immediately begin working on the First Five. Behavior/participation of students is below average.

F (0 points)
Fewer than 60% of students come to class on time, prepared, and immediately begin working on the First Five. Behavior/participation of students is poor.

Daily Theme

Last year, I wanted to changed things up! I wanted to incorporate a new routine into the day, but also something that was fun and changed daily. I came up with the Daily Theme and it was a hit! At the end of the year, students told me that they really enjoyed the Daily Theme because it made the week go faster and they enjoyed the different activities throughout the week. The picture at the bottom of the page shows how I track the days of the week using a Post-it note on a poster. All activities take less than ten minutes.

Music Monday
On Mondays, I play a song for the class and students complete the Musical Text worksheet (pg. 42). I display the lyrics for students. Some weeks I choose the song, and other weeks I allow students to bring in the song (I screen all music in advance). After students complete the worksheet, we review and discuss answers. I like this activity because, like novels, songs tell stories.

News Day Tuesday
On Tuesdays, we discuss some sort of current event. I look for articles relevant to teenagers or pull up wacky news stories to discuss. This activity really brings different points of view and perspectives into the classroom.

Would you Rather? Wednesday
On Wednesdays, I typically read scenarios from various *Would You Rather?* books. Some scenarios are more appropriate for school than others, so I recommend that you screen in advance. Some weeks, I create my own scenarios and other weeks I allow students to create scenarios. I really enjoy this activity because students make excellent points and do a great job supporting their claims.

Teen Topic Thursday
On Thursdays, we have a brief class discussion on school-appropriate topics that teens care about. At the beginning of the year, I had each student write down topics that they were interested in discussing and then I selected the ones that were most appropriate and interesting. Topics included mixed-gender sports teams, new classes that should be offered in school, and teen curfews.

Fun or Frown Friday
The idea of this activity was inspired by a colleague. If students have been good for the week, we have a Fun Friday. This means students get a few minutes of talk time at the end of class and students may bring in a snack. If the behavior for the week did not meet expectations then the class has a Frown Friday. On a Frown Friday, students are not given talk time, they may not bring in snacks, and they may be kept after the bell. I can count on one hand the number of times all of my classes had a Frown Friday this year! Needless to say, students looked forward to Fridays.

Books by Garrett M. Carter:

Not an Oxymoron: Standards-Based Fun in the Classroom! 30 Projects and Activities for Middle School Language Arts (2011)

Common Core Creativity: Language Arts Fun in the Classroom! 30 Projects and Activities for Middle School ELA (2013)

Common Core Galore: Language Arts Fun in the Classroom! 30 Activities for Middle School ELA (2015)

46575114R00035

Made in the USA
Lexington, KY
28 July 2019